This world of world of mine

selected poems

GJV Prasad

This world of mine

selected poems

GJV PRASAD

Hawakal
PUBLISHERS

New Delhi | Calcutta

Hawakal
New Delhi | Calcutta

HAWAKAL PUBLISHERS
70 B/9 Amritpuri, East of Kailash, New Delhi 65
33/1/2 K B Sarani, Mall Road, Calcutta 80

Email info@hawakal.com
Website www.hawakal.com

Cover texture: Shutterstock

Cover designed by Bitan Chakraborty

First edition (paperback) September 2021

ISBN: 978-81-952401-5-9 (paperback)

Price: INR 350 | USD14.99

To
Kamala
and
Shubha
in gratitude for all the poetry

ACKNOWLEDGEMENTS

Many of these poems are new, some old, and most of them have been published already. The following poems were published in my only volume of verse so far, *In Delhi without a Visa* (Delhi: Har Anand, 1996) – 'Desperately Seeking India,' '15th August 1974,' '15th August 1976,' 'Family Poem,' 'Family Poem II,' 'Dynasty,' 'Sati 1,' 'Sati 2,' 'Sati 3,' 'saturday morning ritual,' 'The View,' 'Ishwar Natarajan,' 'where did the masons go,' 'All Abhimanyus,' 'October 31st 1984,' and 'Indiettes' (from which two poems are reproduced here). Many of these were published even earlier: 'Sati 1,' 'Sati 2,' 'Sati 3,' and 'All Abhimanyus' in *Northern Perspective*, 'The View' and 'October 31st 1984' in *Debonair*. Some of the poems from the earlier book have been republished elsewhere and have undergone slight changes over the years.

Among the poems not from my earlier book (the vast majority here), the following have already appeared in various journals and anthologies and websites: 'The

Season of the Cicadas' and 'Godhra-Gujarat' in the *Journal of the Poetry Society of India*, 'Growing Old' and 'Road Kill' in the *Anthology of Indian Poetry II*, edited by Menka Shivdasani at bigbridge.org, 'Thiruvannamalai' in *Direct Path*, 'And Annalakshmi Cried' in *Quesadilla and Other Adventures: Food Poems*, edited by Somrita Ganguly, 'Sunday' in the anthology on 'Sunday,' edited by Somrita Ganguly for Women Empowered (we-view), and 'First Class in Room 016' was published in the e-journal run by the students of the Centre for English Studies, JNU.

❁

My next acknowledgements have to be to the patience shown by my family who have been waiting for me to inflict more poems on the outside world so that they wouldn't have to suffer by themselves. Appa and Amma were very proud of my poetry and happy that I had taken my grandfather's legacy forward. They are not here to see this book.

❁

I must thank all my students and friends who encouraged me to publish my poems so that they could have something to critique. So here you are.

CONTENTS

Desperately Seeking India

In Delhi
Without a visa
In Madras
An Aryan spy

Kashmir's no vacation
They tell me it's a nation
And Punjab wants to die

In Bombay
I'm an invader
In Assam
An exploiting trader

They would throw me
From the hills
Kick me
From the plains

I promise
Never
To mention India again

15th August 1974

we fought for light
we got it
we didn't know
what to make of it

in darkness
there was hope
in light
there is despair

it is many years past midnight
but the blues remain
and we remain
for ever
at little past midnight

15th August 1976

What is this day
That I sit down to write
Poems on my country?

I ought to be in jail

Imprisoned I am
In my own cowardice
But I read the underground press
And burn the papers…

Sorry friends, it has been long,
We've forgotten you in jail,
Having learnt to keep out of it.
We still want our little space
To breathe the noxious gases

Do write your apology letters,
We've already written ours

And this is another…

Family Poem

Amma
ever worried about Appa
finding out
transgressions of children

he always did
and blamed her

Amma
so easily pleased
by minor successes

the smallest of acts
by us her children
even words casually uttered

especially when
directed to Appa

Family Poem II

It was another family night of chats and quizzes
Appa preparing us early for the civil services
I must have been around ten or so
And Appa
As so often
Came out with a pronouncement

We have no religion he said
Adjusting himself in the bed

But we are Hindus,Nattu exclaimed,
A future communist,
One my father would call
A Naxalite sympathizer

You might as well be Gangas or Cauveries
Or better still Ganga-Cauveries, Appa replied
And right now, anyway, a Jamun
Nice enough but a stain on the family honour
Look at the marks you got in your last exam

But you said, Nattu interjected wisely,
Something about us not being Hindus

You have to be a Pakistani to be that
Appa replied, you have to live near the Indus
To be a Hindu

So, in Delhi you are a Jamun

But what about our religion (Nattu still playing safe)

What religion, what ism! Appa exclaimed
What we always had, and have, is a way of life
The Sanathana Dharma
The universal way of life

Must have been a very small universe, Nattu replied
And Appa sighed

That was the night my childhood died
And my Gods haven't survived

Dynasty

Appa could only repair
the ancestral house
his siblings grudged him
in a place where none
of the family lived
nor does

a one car town of no rent

his plot of gold in Delhi
he couldn't mine
and gave my brother
whose loan
cannot meet the cost
of his dream i envy

How Brown Was My Campus

I remember my university
The up-campus
A brown rocky terrain of promise
Radiating heat in the summer
Stone cold in the winter
A road, three hostels, and residences
Of togetherness in the search
For a green and fertile tomorrow

I remember my university
A brown rocky terrain of promise
Of freedoms and new responsibilities
The shock of recognition
Love, understanding, and friendships
Of solidarities forged in the club building
Down-campus dreaming up a present
As well as a future forged in freedom

I remember my university
All the hiccups and misadventures
As also the guns pointed at hostel balconies
And midnight arrests and misidentifications
Of boots on the rocky terrain of promise

Trying to snuff out all intent
The content of debates at dhabas
For an equitable, green and fertile tomorrow

I remember my university
Up-campus still a rocky terrain
Still holding promise and a future with the nilgais
And the peacocks dancing
Slowly greening itself into the ridge
With misadventure and heavy boots of the state
Ending the heavy hubris of a campus
Believing everyone wanted the same

I remember my university
How brown was the campus
And how green we must have been
Learning all the questions
And thinking we would find the answers
That there were answers to find
The more questions we ask
The more questions we need to ask

To know the greening of the campus
Is not a metaphor, not an answer

JNU

This my university
Of depression, frustration, and rage
Of people trying to right wrongs
And wronging rights

This my university
Of stinking loos and potholed roads
Of crowded hostels and shocking hostilities
Of depression, frustration, and rage

This my university
Of constant contestation, endless cups of tea
Midnight meals, love and friendships
Of depression, frustration, and rage

This my university
At war with itself holding together
Each faction fighting for justice and a future
Of depression, frustration, and rage

This my university
Struggling on its way to its promise
Of commitment to a vision to the end
Of depression, frustration, and rage

The Season of the Cicadas (2004)

They strike no terror
Though a woman
Loses control of the wheel
Hits a hydrant floods a street and is the news

The world has changed
New countries new boundaries
New governments new deaths
And Presidents struggling to survive

The years underground
Hasn't changed the mission
Programmed into their genes
All answer the call to death

The dogs of war
Have been loosed round the world
Killing is the habit of faith
Worn with ease

They are killed for pleasure
Boys fry them dogs eat them

Now out in the open
They do not hide or take precautions

They finally found a war they all like
Moral simple and straight they think
Sixty years after
A monument to the dance of death

It is their Woodstock
Days and nights of music
Acting out the message of peace
Moult, mate and die

Photographs from the Middle East
Shock and sicken the soul of a people at war
Waiting for a cause to unite
To die for in reason passion and season

A nation envies the cicadas

Sati 1

when anything went wrong
her grandmother would say
like me a woman born

what could be worse

born her parents' burden
raised to serve others' needs
her marriage had brought them
relief and penury

what could be worse
than to be a woman born

she had failed them badly
for no child called her mother
and he whose presence made
sure of the colour on her
forehead fell ill and died

what could be worse
than to be a woman born
giving happiness to no one

she watched condemned to live
in the shadows the world
indifferent to her needs
unknown when death could give
her all a woman could get
excitement prominence and reverence

what could be worse
than to be a woman born
giving happiness to no one
guilty of your husband's death

she grabbed her only chance
for a place in the sun

Sati 2

What could have been better?

The minute I heard, I packed
Camphor and agarbattis,
And ordered pictures of Goddesses
And other Satis,
And sweets for parshad,
A regular supply of flowers,
And left for the village at once.
A killing was to be made
At the Sati Sthal,
And I intended to be there,
Making the most of it.

And they came in hordes
Like locusts, and stripped
My stall clean;
For once, my supplies lagging behind
The demand, and my cash box
Overflowing.
Oh, the goodness of the Sati!

They bought the pictures of the Devi
Whom the painter had never seen.

They bought the parshad,
And they bought the flowers.
They even bought the ash I said
Was from the funeral pyre
And the earth I said was from the Sthal!
They even bought me drinks
As they bought the stories I told them
About the Sati I had never seen.

What a mela it was,
A religious festival like never before.
You should have been there
To see the faith, the fervour.
The Sati did more for our religion
And region than all the sadhus in action.
Just look at the money we made.

Sati 3

I was there for the chunri ceremony
With my tape recorder and cameraman
Can you believe there was even a stall
Selling bottled drinks
Saved my life
Who could have trusted the water there?

And my God the crowds
Enjoying every second of it
Couldn't believe it was this year
This century this era of liberation
They had made a Goddess of another woman
Burnt alive in this nation

To hint to anyone
That she may have been forced
Was sacrilege
I was making a Devi a woman
Pulling back into the cycle
A soul in liberation

There was condescension
Pats on the backs and betis

There were lewd remarks
Furtive hands
Even in front of the deities
But most of all
An angry assertion of identity
We burn our women alive
How does it matter to you?

The seer the sage of
The mutt said
You have curves in the right places
(The audience sniggered and looked)
I have none
(He had plenty the fat fool)
When we are made unequal
Where is the question
Springing close triumphantly
The old biology trap
As the audience clapped

It solves the problem of widows
Anyhow
He said of the sati

Back at home
Deftly avoiding
Proposals for marriage
I tell my parents the story
They cluck their tongues
And tell me
I have lost touch with our country
That's the trouble with education

My story makes the headlines
The interview a scoop
For days fellow journalists
Cry for the blood of the swami
But soon the story of the girl Roop
Is buried in the inside pages
Along with dowry deaths and minor murders
And the rapes of lower-class girls

But I must rush now
Have to invite so many
You must come at least to the reception
If you can't make it to the ceremony
Come tomorrow anyhow to see the sarees
And the jewellery

Draupadi Said

I beseeched the court,
And they laughed,
Or closed their eyes,
Hanging their heads in shame.

I beseeched you.
You, stealer of clothes,
Responded
By bestowing the longest saree in history,
Which was of no use later.

No, I lie!

Impossible to wash,
It was a never-ending supply
Of rags to clean our huts and palaces,
And you can still see them
Clothing some poor soul's modesty.

I lie again, as I lied earlier
When I said it was of no use *later*.

Of what use was it then

When
All I wanted was you the God
To mete out justice
Summary, summary justice.

I was a fool
To expect such –
Anything was too much –
From men or Gods

Hey Ram

You came, so young, a God, and broke the bow;
I watched, so young, my Lord, my heart my foe.
The role became me so well, a demure wife;
With my master always, I said, my Ayodhya, my life.
Ever aware of your place and duty,
A good family man but better on a committee;
Love to you was a procedural lapse,
All kith' and kin potential traps.

Your rules called, and I proved to be fire.

But as ever you played a different game,
Every excuse I thought for you still so lame.

Even today, when they light the lamps, I feel the flames.

What then was the meaning, what was your cause?
And what did the world gain by my loss?

Kumkumappoo

You don't really need it
My mother said
Many cannot even afford a strand
Or take a stand

And you know our nation
So much adulteration
They'll drink our blood
And sell us tinted water
For transfusion
Saps your faith I tell you

Sorry got carried away
A pinch is all you need
If it is genuine stuff
If not it will only be colour
Simply colour without flavour
You would rather do without
So don't tell me I didn't warn you

As I was saying
Only if you want and can afford it
Add a little pinch at the end

The flavour of India
It may be from Kashmir or Spain
Nothing like a pinch of saffron I tell you
To truly finish an Indian sweet

Your grandmother would say
As she added the saffron
Now it is fit for the Gods
And to me it has always been
The fragrance of heaven
The flavour of a tradition
But a pinch is all you need
India can afford no more

saturday morning ritual

relieved of the weight
of the jewellery
i haven't bought you
head soaked in oil
my wife, you wait
for my first faux pas of the day

being male and a husband
for me there is no escape

Partitions

Yours Ours killed, maimed, looted
Yours Ours raped, tortured, gloated
Yours Ours cut your our limbs off
Yours Ours still feel the phantom pain

The phantom never dies
Old jungle saying
Nor does the pain
The missing limbs
Actually still alive
Still hacking still hacked

Every drop of blood
Sprouts
Into a hundred blooms of hatred
Thorns, swords, sickles, bullets, and bombs
A land divided in bloodshed
Will split and spill till the last
Unless the Gods give you
A common enemy

WhatsAppery

We all belong to such groups
We would love to get out of
But don't, for various reasons
But mainly to know
What the other side thinks

A woman just has to say
It is a man's world and horribly so
And the WhatsAppery will begin

What do you mean?

Take the case of harassment reported today
The girl isn't going to get any justice

Why should we believe the girl?
Why do you assume there will be no justice?
Maybe she is simply making a false allegation
And the man is innocent
Maybe he will get justice!

I am sorry for intervening here
But women don't go around making false allegations

Speak for yourself
I haven't said anything about you
Many women make false allegations
And mess up the lives of men
This is usually the case

I am sorry, I don't understand
How you can say such a thing
With such confidence

I have headed a department
I know what I am talking about
I know a case
A man known to a friend of mine
Whose wife left him and whose children
Don't even talk to him
Just because of a false allegation

Sorry, how do you know it was false?
Did the enquiry committee find it so?

Huh, don't act dumb!
The system is screwed
Skewed against men
He was held guilty
But there were no witnesses
She was lying
She hadn't been promoted I think
And this was her revenge

Sorry, but there are usually no witnesses
For such events; there must have been enough

Evidence to find him guilty

You will say so, you are a woman
We have seen how women exploit the laws
How they rule the world now
All men held guilty
Until they can establish
Their innocence
Women are dangerous in the workplace

Sorry, what did you say?
I am so upset at the turn this discussion
Has taken
Women are dangerous?
We women in this group
And hopefully some of the men too
Object strongly.
How can you even say such things?

Because women are so,
I can give you statistics
And case studies

What nonsense
Ask your wife ask your daughter
If they feel safe going out
At any time
Whether they ever feel
That they are not being gazed at
As prey

I have trained them to be brave

And practical
They can take care of themselves
And they know how to dress
And when to go out!

With your permission, of course

They know who knows best about things
As I do
I ask them for recipes
And bow to their expertise in the kitchen
And the household in general
We are not westerners
We are Indians who know how to revere women

Can't believe this
And the men in the group
Are silent!

The fact is that women
Have filed false dowry cases
Have accused men of rape
If a relationship doesn't end in marriage
The laws are so skewed
We men walk around in fear

Oh really? Men walk around in fear!
Not even the fake news cell
Would dare to circulate that!
Your words drip with the power
The entitlement of men
In this men's world

You can do what you want in your house
And outside
The casual sexism
The place you allot to women
The harassment you think
Is camaraderie in the workplace
And the perks of a shared space
God
You guys are sick
And I am not even speaking of rapes and murders
The acid attacks and the videos
The threats and the violence
The silencing

WHAT SILENCING? NONE OF US
HAVE
BEEN
ABLE
TO SILENCE YOU!
NO WONDER YOU ARE FULL OF THIS PASSION
NEVER FOUND THE RIGHT MAN!

This is our world! This is us!
Not all men are like this
You may think
But how is that an answer
Other than WhatsAppery

Just Reality

And will you marry her
And make her an honest woman
Asked the judge of the rapist

She felt violated all over again

The judge felt no remorse
After all rape was allowed in marriage
And he could do what he wanted
And she have the position of a wife
Win-win all around!

Humanity drowned in blood
Torn to shreds by barbarity

No said the rapist's lawyer
Milord, now it would be bigamy
He would have loved to marry her then
Now he is a married man with children
How can he marry his prey of earlier times

Yes, thought the judge

He has another woman now to rape

This is fate, young woman
You were at the wrong place at the wrong time
Tempted him too early in his life
A little later, and you could have been his wife

He is a respectable man
Wont it be best to reach a settlement
Make him pay for his act
He said

And laughed at his own joke

And Annalakshmi Cried

Every morsel you waste
Adds another drop of tear
To Annalakshmi's eyes
As she mourns by the river
My grandfather said

An American friend said
His mother made him eat
By asking him to imagine me
Starving in India
Or Africa

But how would that have helped
I asked him
Only made you bigger and stronger
To put me in my place
He didn't know
He had never asked his mom
And she was dead now
And in any case
This Indian didn't look
He starved ever

Maids used to bring lunch
For the rich kids in class
And the smell of eggs and oranges

Still reminds me of school
Curd rice of home
While I longed for samosas and coke

We went without sugar
For a year or two
And rice was difficult to find
The green revolution
A distant dream
Not yet a nightmare

They poured milk into the seas
Elsewhere
And let grains rot in the fields
The same world I would think
And when they did send
Some across
We hated them for it

I remember when potatoes
Meant a feast
We were the privileged ones
Whose dustbins others
Would forage and envy
The one who got more
Snatching it from dogs

Source locally they say
Sustainability they intone
Where there is clean water
And fertile fields
Some can do so
Because they can
Others will do as ever
Because they can't

The View

Gold alchemizing my mood
I watched the rays
Fill the valley below
The town for once looking beautiful

The old man brushed past me
Bent to his daily chore
Locked into himself
So I said look

Look at the sunset

He picked up some more twigs
Perrilously close to the edge
Looked up and sighed
What's so special Babu
You can't eat it can you?

For Sumana

What do the poor eat,
What do they eat?
Asked her nephew
I saw them eating grass
In a photo
Eating grass like cows!
Are cows poor too?
Asked her nephew
Is that why
You turned into a tree
To feed them plenty
And forever?
Is that why
You want me
To turn into a vessel
Of plenty and forever?
And where is the cow
Of plenty and forever?
Please don't turn into a tree
The nephew pleaded
To his aunt
We will find the magic words
You will write them
And there will be no rich
No poor

Growing Old

In English he became someone's old man early
It took time in his Indian languages

But as he grew older and more respected not in
English
English kept him young and with it

His wisdom he gained in years not in English
Alzheimer's stared at him in English

Soon he ealized
He was growing old and unwanted
In English
As also not in English

Her Story

This is my story
And you can't write it
She cautioned

No, this is not the one
About the senior writer
Who thought feminist writers
Were available
And was disappointed in them

No, this is not even the one
About the lying professors
Who didn't know how else
To get a woman student
Into a relationship

They are fairly common
Don't make interesting stories

This is about a friend
Someone you know
Who was lonely then
For people from home

In the big city

He would spend time
With a lot of us
Because we were a gang
His friend from home
Was a part of

No story, yet, I said

Listen, he won a scholarship
To go abroad
And came to spend his last evening
With us and no one was in the hostel
Except me

So, we went to India Gate
For an ice cream
The first ever time he had treated anyone
A cop comes along
We were sitting there
Licking our ice cream in peace

No licking allowed he said
Chalo thane
Police station
He repeated
No shame at all nowadays

"But we are only having ice cream!"

Is that what you call it now
Wonder what your parents will say
Having ice cream in public
Disturbing peace with public nuisance

"But this is an ice cream!"

Hut, don't make me look! No shame,
No shame!
Come to the station you bugger
You go home miss

"What? Why is she allowed to go home?"

Yes, why should I?
Take me to the station too!

No, no, miss. Go home to your family
You look like a respectable lady
Not like this lout. You shouldn't be here
With such a man.

"I told her so, only she insisted on a treat!"

Chup! Shut up, blaming the woman
For what you wanted to do.
As if a respectable girl like her
Would have asked you for this!

But, police sir, I did!
This guy is a miser, the first time ever
That he has treated me!

Miser, uh. Let us see how miserly
He is! Chal, let us go to the station.

"Or?"

Or give me some money.

Let us go the station,
It will be fun!

"Are you mad?
Tomorrow, I am leaving the country!
I can't afford to go to the station,
Do you have any money?"

What?

Arrey! You are asking her for money!
Take out your purse, you miser,
You lout, you useless fellow
Take out your purse.

"Sir, sirji! Please don't take all the money!
I have to go to the airport tomorrow
I need to pay my fare."

Chal, take this. You will remember this day forever
And thank it was me and no other
Policeman who caught you
Licking ice cream in public!

The ice creams melted, unlicked,

As they left in a hurry
The policeman right
The day never forgotten

His girlfriends never knew
Why he wouldn't take them to India Gate
For an evening of ice cream!

Kai Visiri

I am a fanatic of fans
Not a fan of fanatics
Do not fan the flames of prejudice
Nor fan the pride of the powerful
Rather fan the sweat off the labourer
Fan to sleep the tired, dead from work

The Sahibs have moved on from fans
The punkah wallahs obsolete as their fans
But the hand fans see us through hot days and nights
Of the powerless, each fan a story
Each swing a song, a sigh, a smile of memory
Do you remember the night of the stars?
Of the meteor shower?
The night wasn't hot but still
And we had run out of fans
So you made one out of paper and it was so much fun
That all of us had folded paper fans as we watched
The dark light up for us
The joy we felt that night

Tatha always wanted the electric fan on one
Like a maiden slowly fanning a king we would say

Today, the invertor ensures the hand fan is on the wall
Another decoration piece along with
Large brass vessels and tall metal lamps
Reminding us of the exquisiteness of our pasts
Reassuring in their wisdom that when all else fails
The hand fan will bring the winds of change.

Road Kill

The streets rage in Delhi

They circle round your throat
Like pythons
In heat and cold
Rain and shine

Arterial and venal

A man killed a bus driver the other day
Another, a taxi driver, raped his customer
And then burnt her
A policeman simply picked up a brick
Not having been issued a revolver

Everyone is in a hurry
Everyone on a tight short leash
The red light always ready
To beat you before you begin

Stopping the poor
And daring to stop the rich

Someone has to get it

The streets rage in Delhi

behold the dark

who could believe

that light
could end life

that intense brightness
could illuminate
the essential darkness
of humans

perhaps
there is a lesson in the dark

you hold hands
when you can't see
with people
you don't know

and come together as a world

(written for the post-atom bomb world)

Ishwar Natarajan

Appa said the other day
That Ishoo you
Must be a saint reborn
To live out your unspent days
Your parents the blessed ones

A soul so noble
He said
Beyond thought and action
Inspiring in your parents
A selfless dedication
To all special children

Ishoo you
Appa said
Are a saint reborn

But the doctors only know
The brain that can't
And the unworldly body
That will grow

This was Nattu

This was Nattu
I said sifting through
The ashes and bones

No, snapped Gopi,
His lifelong friend,
Only something
To remember him by

We cast a leaking pot of memories
Into the ocean
Right next to the sanctuary
He had made his own

Like waves in the ocean are we
Said someone
Always there
But only for moments
For ever and almost never

The rest of the ashes

We carried in a plastic bag
To the hills he so loved
And immersed in the holy river

The plastic bag retrieved
At the last minute
("Let us not add to the pollution")
Had some traces of ashes still

Nattu always wanted to live life to the full
Till the end

We washed the bag out
In the cleansing waters
Hope he breaks free of the chain
Someone said
As the river rushed to meet the ocean

So that was that

Why are they holding this havan
Asked Poonam
Why are they talking of him
As if to remember him
Is an effort

Four years have gone by
And finally gone
Are the dark circles
So cruelly painted
Around her eyes

Why are they praying
For his soul
And our peace
When he is here with me
As he always has and will
Poonam asked
In bewilderment

He is here
And that is that

where did the masons go

the marble breaking backs
of the doomed men
the sleepless ceaseless toil
the deepening sores the ruptured boils
the whips the epidemics the starvation
love was a grave business
in this nation

when he looked at the tomb
the King knew he'd be remembered
so what if his sons
wanted him dismembered

All Abhimanyus

Wildly the pigeon fluttered into the pane
that still divides though you may see afar

It beat its head in vain

Once in a glasshouse you had better learn
To throw stones or bear the inner heat

A Poem for Stephanos

The world speaks in tongues
Written in different strokes
In a register in Cyprus
In what was once a church
A mosque and a church again

All origins are in translation

I see Christ in a monastery
The colour ageing
A glowing dark to a pale white
Around the world
The word in a palette

The word is translation

It is an old land
Of ancient peoples
Of myths and history
Celebrating the ordinary
Aphrodite among the cats

Each age a translation

A Punjabi I met in the market
Thought he was in Cyprus USA
Though he wasn't paid in dollars
And the ghit-phit didn't sound the same
He was still in some promised land

Nations are born in translation

Our origins may be across the boundaries
Of violence and madness
Blood may seemingly call
To villages by the river
And our valleys were always green

Memory is translation

People move with remembered rituals
Walking on burning coals
Piercing their bodies
To satisfy to thank
Their Gods of translation

Rowing with Fate

We are all born
Sentenced to Life
Sometimes
We want it commuted
To Death

We float down the river
Rowing with Fate

We are all born
Sentenced to Life
Sometimes
We want it commuted
To Death

We float down the river
Of life
With what floats down
With us
Till

Rivers die
Hills disappear
Forests burn

We curse Fate

In a travelling cage
We share at times with others

We think we are
On what could have been
Great journeys

If only it were our Fate

31ˢᵗ October 1984

I watched him burn

The other time I watched someone burn
he was dead already

It was a picnic that time
for it isn't every day that you get
to attend the funeral of a friend
who deserved to die and much earlier
a great soul eaten into by cancer

He was burning beautifully they said

As we waited for the skull to explode
in the heat his brother smiling
at the bargain he had struck for the wood
as some of his friends went for a swim
and others took a boat ride on the Jamuna

Corpses are tied down to avert mishaps
and skulls cracked open to enable people
to catch buses they'd otherwise miss
and of course stories are told with smiles

of corpses coming alive early enough
to be saved from fiery death

Unlike brides wilfully burnt
for being unable to bring more dowry
or abetted to suicides by helpful in laws
keeping alive another kind of sati
in this non-violent vegetarian country
that likes the stench of cooked human flesh

He had stopped shrieking long ago
and the mob raced after another victim
as an American TV cameraman filmed the corpse
for posterity and breakfast TV

From 'Indiettes'

1

Degeneration Gap

Thaatha wore his kudumi for long
(hiding it in turbans)
not daring to chop it off
till his father died
but not of seeing his cropped hair

decades later he was to yell at us
call us hippies
complain of the kaliyugam
for growing our hair long

2

Statement III

There is no hope
No hope
For they say

With the rains

Come the floods
And after the floods
The drought

You either die with water
Or you die without

Godhra-Gujarat

The girl who fainted in fear
Before the flames seared her
Suffocated
By a weight
Heavier than smoke
And turned
To ashes and bones

What were her last thoughts?

What was the last breath
As the mob lobbed kerosene bottles
And set the coach on fire

Did she sigh
The name of her God
Like the mahatma

The mob so secure in its fury

Did the people with fire
Take the name of their Lord
The sacrifices offered
At the altar of their cause

Or did that not matter a bit

As the flames reached the heaven
Of one faith or the other

Blood, hate, and tears,
They must have sweated
God
What is God to make of them?

And what can writers do
What could anyone have written then
The poetry went up in smoke

II

And then the people of faith
Exacting revenge in numbers
For sins committed or omitted
For being there

What did they think they were
Foreigners in this land of temples
Have to be taught once and for all
Where they belong –
Not here not here
If here only for our sport

The blood leaked into the roads
Dissolved the ashes
Gathered in puddles
Printed itself onto feet

And tramped the beat
Of journalists and TV crews
As murderers strutted into view

It was good said the teacher
Now we have our pride back
You know what Ghazni did
To our temples and Gods
We have paid him back
Ten eyes for an eye
All thirty two for a tooth

Ah glorious it was
He said
The making of our Gujarat
The water of mother Narmada
And their blood on our hands
What more can we pray for
Blessed now is our land

We, the men of God

What are we to make of all this
And what could anyone have written then
The poetry tainted beyond belief

Gujarat 2005

Taught them a lesson
He said
They will never forget
A pity most of them are dead

It doesn't matter
Others will remember
In the ghettoes
Don't want them here

But don't worry
We do business with them
Money is money
We cannot let Gujarat die

Post-Trauma

sometimes life is a dog's
bared teeth
and bounding energy
who can know
its smile from its snarl
life is interpretation
of god's will
in dog's deed

First Class in Room 016

No longer that young, but still young
Enough for life to be an adventure
Of possibilities…

Even, if looking at others,
some
Feel they are already behind,
Small town, old fashioned dregs of history;

Cursed be their loving parents
(oh, why couldn't they let go?).
Their beloved parents.
So embarrassing, so…

A class
Full of (silent) expectation,
Most will find their voice;
Some their destiny.

Room 016
Never disappoints those that seek

Bhakti poem 1

Take me God/dess
Mingle in me
Let me dissolve in you

This world of bodies
Of senses of desire
Of skin and touch
Of tongue and taste
Of sight and delight
Is but a happy reflection
Of me and you together
Of me in you
Of you in me
Take me now God/dess

Sunday

Never on a Sunday,
She crooned into my adolescent ears
Everyday is not a Sunday
Became suddenly a welcome mantra

There are people for whom
There are no Sundays
No days of rest
The women in my home didn't have any

Nor did we children
We played all day and
Whined over the homework
And fought for space

There were workers
For whom Sundays were special
They could find employment
When masters were home

Sometimes Sundays were a pain
When fathers were home
Aware of the shortcomings
Of children they tasked all day

Sundays reminded our parents
Of religion and ritual
Look at the Christians
They go once a week to their church

If all was good with the world
Why wasn't every day a Sunday
Except that the girl crooned
Never on a Sunday

Maya

So, this is Maya
I look at her

So, this is Maya
She looks at me

When dreams touch
New worlds are born

All is Maya

Two Writers at JNU

1

The room was FULL bursting at the
Seams
Eager young faces turning towards
The Queen

Her reputation
Must have come at a cost
Oh, how she must have fought
This poet of love and loss

Which Indian middle-class woman
Had said the things she had
In print
In poetry?

She truly needed no
Introduction;
Whichever language she dreamt in,
So did they!

Look at you girls, she said,
No fashion-sense!

I am sure you don't know
How to cook, either.

They sat stunned
As she took off on
How to get a man to love
And stay in love for a while

Dress up, dress up,
She said
And where is your make-up?
And learn to cook

Feminism has spoilt you all

It was before the age of the selfie
They had had plans for photographs
For Autographs and a long session
Of poetry

2

He is what they call now
A senior poet
He was one
Even then

A friend and a lovely man
He had agreed to speak
And read from his poetry

Ambitious faculty on the make

Had called the Rector
To preside
The poet, one of stature

And what do you do
Asked the Rector
Leaning back
Taking a puff from his pipe

I write poetry
(He was to write novels much later)

No, no.
What do you really do?

He is a senior officer in the police
I said
The Rector choked
In laughter

After some water
And pats on the back
He straightened up and
Jokes apart, what do you really do?
He asked!

Mothers' Day

A mother is born
With her child

Not Krishna…

But why not Krishna

Taken away at birth
Delivered to a new mother
Care perhaps even breast giver
Nurturer
Nursing him
Through illnesses
Feeding him to health
Berating him
To the straight and
The broad minded

The sperm not his father's
The egg not his mother's
But making them
Mom and dad

But no, not Krishna

The sperm very much the father's
The egg very much the mother's
But born to a womb giver
Nourished by her blood
And comforted by the security
Of her heartbeat
The baby yearns to hear
Later

The mother's child
The father's child

But the cord
Binds the child to another
With the rented womb

Birth-giver
But not the mother

Not her day …

Poetry

Why does poetry make so much sense to me
When I never know what the poets mean
Why does poetry give me so much energy
When it takes so much effort to read

Tiruvannamalai

The hill
Overlooks the aspirations
Pointing upwards
Reaching outwards
Immersed in its surroundings

It is
Earth and sky
Light and dark
As likely to dissolve
As to evolve

All states of being
All being states
All being
All
Being one

Recognise
Says the hill
Overlooking all
Giving succour
To all
Being one with all
All
Being one

Starbucks

the frappe foams
laughter
of an office anecdote

shy smiles of a first
shall we call it
a date

an older couple waiting
for someone
with crosswords

couples on the way home
with stragglers hoping
the coffee would get them
there

Edible Woman

Shall I call you my crisp samosa
My aloo parantha or masala dosa
Delhi wafers or my aloo tikki
Aloo chaat or urulaibajji?

I mean to say I can snack
On you any time
And time and again
You are so maddening
Loveable desirable
And incredible

And clog my arteries
And my heart beats so
Rapidly frantically
Trying to find normal
In a world that is you

You stop my heart
You jump start my life
You are so stunningly
Addictive attractive
I can see nothing but you
My jangiri my halwa
My burfi my desi ghee
Besan laddoo

Election Strategies: Shining India

I woke up one day to see India Shining
The papers said so in bold that morning
Cleansed of those who had kept India pining

For the rising of saviours with swords
Trishul, chakkoos, churies, or iron rods
Who would shed the blood of others for our Gods

I remembered a day in 1984
When the Prof said we have shown them the door
Either you belong to us or to an alien shore

We've taught them a lesson he said
Like all the Muslims who in my village are dead
We showed them in 47 when our soil turned red

Just do it often enough times
Scrub hard and long to remove all the Staines
Who think our land is open for their religious gains

We have unleashed the Hindu tide
We have restored the Hindu pride
We have saved the Hindu bride

Yearly blood-letting keeps the nation glowing
The interests in our vote banks growing
We are the ones who keep India Shining

We never had it so good said the ad
And of course they never had is so bad
Just beat Pak at cricket Ganguly lad

The Long March

There they were on the roads
Trudging along as they do
To a home that is nowhere
No vehicles to take them there

There they were
On railway tracks of despair
The trains didn't run
They were told
Till one ran over them
Resting on the sleepers
Their blood seeping into the earth
Their home their final resting place

There they were dying on the roads
Dead on the railway tracks
On our TV screens
And our social media
Their rough calloused feet
Bleeding all over our news sites

There they were on the roads
All over the place and dying where they wished
Why couldn't they be herded properly
Anchors asked

Why no arrangements had been made
Food and shelter for the night and water
And loos
Not that they needed clean toilets
They would dirty them soon
Even if some of them cleaned ours

There they were on the roads
On railway tracks
And our screens
Their world on their heads
As if bloody and thirsty bands
Had chased them across the border
In a new Partition of the land

Families stuck together on the roads
Fearing rapists, traffickers, and thieves
Being killed off by good old fashioned
Thirst, hunger, and disease
Mothers nursing dead babies
And infants nuzzling their dead mothers
On our screens
Our fascinated horrified fascinated gaze

There they were marching on the roads
Accepting without smiles
Water and food and guilt money
Too little too late to keep them going
Till they came back
To do our jobs
To run our world
As we watched them on our screens